Contents

Written by Richard Marson and Anne Dixon

BBC

Blue Peter

Annual 2006

Pedigree

Published by Pedigree Books Limited, Beach Hill House, Walnut Gardens, Exeter, Devon, EX4 4DH.
Email: books @pedigreegroup.co.uk By arrangement with the BBC.
BBC logo and Blue Peter logo are registered trademarks of the British Broadcasting Corporation, and are used under licence.
Blue Peter word Logo © BBC 1985. Blue Peter ship logo © BBC 1963. BBC logo © BBC 1996

£7.99

Hello

And welcome to our thirty-fifth Blue Peter book. So much has happened since the last that it's been a huge challenge to fit everything in. So where do we begin?

This was our first year of running three times a week on BBC1 and five times a week on the CBBC Channel. That's a lot of extra work so, what with that and Liz taking a few weeks off to have her baby, we decided it was time to welcome Blue Peter presenter number 30, Zoe Salmon. Zoe's arrival made headlines and you can follow her through her first day on page 56.

We also said hello to Blue Peter's newest pussy cat, Smudge, after we decided to retire Kari and Oke, who had been with us for an incredible 13 years. You can read more about Smudge and have a go at making your own version of television's top cat on page 76. On page 62, there's news of yet another new arrival – Liz's baby, Dexter. Not to be outdone, in May Meg presented Matt – and Blue Peter – with her first litter of puppies.

There!

Our saddest moment was breaking the news of Simon's decision to leave us after over six fantastic years on the programme. We knew we'd really miss him and that he'd be a tough act to follow, but we think we've found the best man for the job in Gethin Jones. You can read about some of his first assignments in this book.

Other highlights included the day we celebrated 4000 editions of Blue Peter, our first interactive shows, and our James Bond Special. You can see us all glammed up at the beginning and end of this book. See how many of our other favourite moments you recognise on this page – the answers are on page 109.

We hope you enjoy looking back over a brilliant Blue Peter year – and that you'll be watching all the many adventures we've got planned in the months to come!

Sing A Song Of Matt

I've had so many challenges on Blue Peter, but this was one of my most exciting. I'd been asked if I could write and produce a pop song for Christmas. I've always enjoyed music and I play very basic guitar and keyboards, but this was in a different league altogether.

I knew I'd need some expert help and I found it in Mike Stock, a pop music genius who has been the brains behind loads of hit singles – it was Mike who launched Kylie on her massively successful career. His advice was to the point: "Three minutes isn't a lot of time. You need to tell a story."

"Keep it simple. And be prepared to spend many hours on the mixing of the track - this can make or break a record."

With Mike on my side, next I needed a band to perform whatever I came up with. When Mikey, Andrew, Nikk and Chris – otherwise known as Phixx – agreed to front the single, I was in business!

My plan was to write a song all about Father Christmas and, over the next few days, wherever I was I kept trying out new words and ideas. I decided to start the song with a Christmassy choirboy solo and to have some children to help out my "Yo ho ho!" chorus. At long last I'd worked out my lyrics and my tune. It was pretty tense waiting for Mike to deliver his verdict – but he seemed impressed. He made a few tweaks and suggested some lyric changes before telling me:

"Well done! Now the hard work really begins..."

And he was right. We recorded and mixed the track at a top London studio. The Phixx boys were first to arrive. They liked the track and were soon stuck in. But I hadn't realised just how long it would take until I'd got a vocal performance I was pleased with.

Next, BBC Choirboy of the Year, Tom Jesty, and the boys from Pilgrims School arrived to add their contributions.

It all took hours – and then the all-important mixing began, adding backing vocals and effects, setting the level of each take we'd recorded, and bringing the complete sound together. It was early the next morning before we'd finished.

Just before Christmas, Phixx and the boys were in the Blue Peter studio to perform the song live. Only afterwards did we let on who had written it!

I was on cloud nine – I'd achieved a lifetime ambition and what's more, I'm determined it won't be the last song I write. Watch out Robbie Williams!

Father Christmas

This one's for you to let you know how
much we all do love you, Father Christmas.
It's thanking you for all the things
you bring.
Our gift to you is what we're gonna sing.
And it's called Father Christmas.

With his elves, he's stacking shelves
With things that they have made
for us for Christmas.
He's checking off his list and making sure
that nothing's missed for us this Christmas
Selecting from his range of bright red suits,
He'll squeeze into his jacket and his boots.
Pulls on his hat and fluffs his beard so
white.
They'll keep him warm as he flies
through the night.
Here comes Father Christmas.

We're singing…
Ho ho ho!
He's taking care of Christmas.
Ho Ho Ho!
He knows everybody's wishes.
It's his job, yes he's the man,
Relax, he's got it all in hand.
It's his business, he's Father Christmas.

The wait has gone, it's been a year.
Christmas Eve at last is here, it's
Christmas.
Tonight's the night, it's clear and bright,
The reindeer ready to take flight this
Christmas.
He'll wait until the last eyelid is closed
When everyone's asleep then off he goes,
Stopping off for tipples and mince pies,
Flying with our presents across the skies
Here comes Father Christmas!

Written by: Matt Baker   Performed by: Phixx

Disco Fever

If your dolls have glitzy clothes but nowhere to boogie on down, here's how to create a disco from an empty grocery carton.

1. Cut off the top flaps and one of the long sides of a carton and keep these pieces to one side. Cover the box in pretty paper or material. Bubble wrap looks very effective as wall covering especially if you paint the smooth side before attaching it to the box. Cut pieces that will cover both inside and outside the box. Attach by gluing the box and carefully laying the bubble wrap in position.

2. To create a luxury quilted look on one wall, cut a piece of wadding the same size and some shiny material a little larger. Cover the wadding with the material and glue the wadding side to the box. Use a pen to mark dots in a diamond fashion approximately 5cm apart. Carefully use a bradawl to make a hole where the dots are. Push paper fasteners through all the holes opening them out on the other side. If you have enough material use it to cover the outside of the box.
The floor is the large side of the box. Paint it or cover it with sticky-backed plastic before slotting into position.

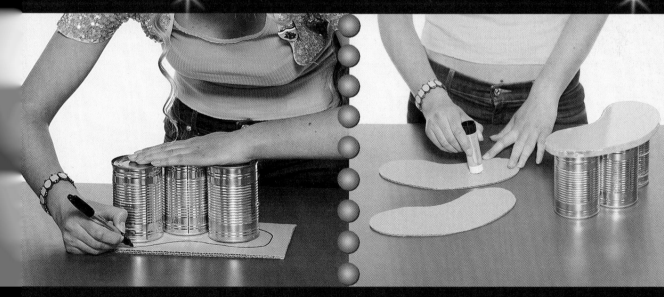

3. Disco dancers get extremely thirsty so find 3 empty cans and turn them into a juice bar. Rinse and then dry the cans and be very careful not to cut yourself on any sharp edges.
Then make the top and bottom of the bar. Lay the cans in a curved shape on a piece of card. Draw around the cans leaving a border of roughly 1cm. You should end up with a kidney shape to use as a template to cut out 5 identical shapes in thick card.

4. To make the bottom of the bar, glue 2 shapes together and use 3 to make the top. Paint or cover these with sticky-backed plastic. Glue the cans in between the top and the bottom of the bar.

5. Stools are empty yoghurt pots painted silver. Find a piece of card and draw around the base of the yoghurt pot. Cut out the circle and cover it with a piece of wadding followed by a piece of fabric. Glue the cushion in place on the bottom of the yoghurt pot.

6. To complete the bar area make a fresh orange juice machine from an empty spill-proof water bottle. Cut the bottle roughly in half. Then cut off the bottom section about 1cm up. Scrunch up some orange tissue paper and push it into the top section of the bottle.

7. Use sticky tape to glue the bottom of the bottle to the top section. When it's turned upside down and sitting on the bar it should look very effective.

8. To make a sofa, find a suitable box and cover one of the long sides with wadding. Then cover the whole box in fabric and if the corners look a little messy glue or stitch on some braid.

9. The table base is a small empty can and the table top is a circle of thick card covered with sticky-backed plastic. Glue the top to the bottom of the can and allow to dry.

10. Make tiny glasses of juice from modelling clay rolled into sausage shapes. Wrap clear film around them. Small sections of painted cocktail sticks make the perfect sized drinking straws.

11. The DJ's sound desk is cut from the bottom section of an extra-large plastic milk bottle. Draw a line beneath the handle all the way round and carefully cut along it. Cover with bubble wrap leaving the top plain.

13. The decks are made from small boxes covered in silver holographic paper. The records are circles of shiny black card with small circles of coloured card stuck in the centres. Glue the records onto the decks. The controls are made from another small box covered with black paper. Use a silver marker to

14. The arms of the decks which play the records are made from 2 cocktail sticks coloured using a silver pen. The arms are attached to the deck by cutting off the tiny closure parts from an egg carton. Push the cocktail sticks into these sections and put tiny beads onto the other ends.

15. When the arms are glued to the corners of the decks with the cocktail sticks hanging over the records they look very realistic.

16. The dance floor is a circle of card and a raised section is made from an empty cheese box. Cover both with glittery paper or sticky-backed plastic.

17. Make a set of multi coloured disco lights from sections of a sweet tube. Cut off 3.5cm lengths and cover them in foil. Each light needs to have discs covering both ends – one to match in silver and the other in a bright disco light.

18. The light holders are 2 sections of bendy straws. Cut each straw 3cm either side of the bendy part and join the 2 sections to make a U shape. To connect the holder to the light push a cocktail stick all the way through and this will enable them to swivel.

19. Cut a length of strong card that is a little wider than your disco and cover it in shiny paper. This will become a small section of ceiling. Attach the disco lights and then tape the ceiling on top of your disco. If you can find a mirror bauble this will make a brilliant disco ball.

20. Finally, put your dolls in the disco and turn up the music – turn it up loud!

Blue Peter

Konnie Huq

Anybody who knows me well will tell you that, even though I wasn't really cut out to be an all-action girl, I'll always have a go! These pictures bring back some very chilly memories of what we called our New Year nightmare.

I think it was somebody in the Blue Peter office's idea of a joke. You know – it's the beginning of January, freezing cold, when most people are happiest curled up inside, preferably near a fire or radiator. So why not get the Blue Peter team to spend two days in the winter countryside learning survival techniques?

Working with Matt, I learnt to make fires, put up a (supposedly) waterproof shelter using twigs and leaves, and build a fully practical boat – again using very basic ingredients. It was all a bit like a giant-sized Blue Peter make! Surprisingly, it turned out to be a lot of fun – and we were kept too busy to think about the cold. That's what I love about Blue Peter - there's never a dull moment.

The Magic of Christmas

Like millions of others, I'd often watched **Blue Peter** at Christmas, enjoying all the traditional ingredients of carols, presents and singing and dancing. Little did I know that I would be introduced to viewers as part of that special programme. The idea was that I'd pop out of a large Christmas present, on which the tag would say "OPEN NOW", and surprise everybody.

Luckily I wasn't alone in feeling like the new kid on the block. Gethin (who had actually auditioned for Blue Peter on the same day as me) was just as nervous – and he wasn't even appearing as himself. That's because it is something of a Blue Peter tradition for new presenters to make an uncredited first appearance before their official debut on screen. Gethin was all dressed up as Father Christmas. He'd be coming through our totaliser doors, well hidden beneath the layers of his suit and his thick white beard. The only clue to his true identity – the Welsh accent!

So when did I make my sneaky first appearance? A few days earlier I'd joined Matt on a filming trip to the ancient town of Nuremberg in Germany. Matt's mission was to visit the fabulous Christmas market there to find some replacement figures for our Christmas crib, which had been bought at the market way back in 1965 by the presenters of the time.

The market is famous for its spiced gingerbread and Matt helped to make some before selling it on a stall. My little moment in the film was to play his first customer. The gingerbread was delicious and the whole experience really put me in a Christmassy mood.

Blue Peter

Back at Television Centre, a whole day was spent in the studio rehearsing and recording all the big song and dance numbers we planned to show on the Christmas programme. I hadn't realised just how much hard work goes into getting these right but, having appeared in loads of shows when I was growing up, I loved every glitzy minute of it.

One of my favourites was Rudolph the Red Nosed Reindeer – done in pantomime style with me as Prince Charming, Konnie as Cinderella, and the boys as two hilariously ugly Ugly Sisters.

Another corner of the studio was turned into a winter wonderland. The only problem was that the shiny white floor was just about as slippery as real ice – not ideal when you're dancing!

Simon really went for it when he took to the mic to belt out Shake a Tail Feather. There was so much energy in this number – we all had a real laugh performing it.

Fast forward to two weeks later and the climax of our show – singing a carol with hundreds of children crowded into our studio. In just 24 packed minutes, viewers had seen my official introduction, enjoyed our song and dance spectacular, and had that first glimpse of Gethin in disguise. It was a very happy day and we both agreed that from now on, the magic of Christmas would mean even more to us than ever before.

From Freeze to FEAST

One thing my time on Blue Peter has shown me is that we live in a truly incredible world – one that's full of extremes. Take two of my favourite filming assignments this year – starting with the trip Zoe and I made to the land of the midnight sun or Iceland. On the surface, Iceland may be cold, but underneath it is quite literally on fire thanks to the molten rock or magma which flows just beneath the ground.

All over Iceland, you find volcanoes, hot springs and geysers – huge walls of steam and water which spurt up from the ground.

I loved the time I spent dog sledding. I may be a one-dog man, but this pack were beauties and surprisingly fast over the ice.

Meanwhile, Miss Salmon managed to catch a salmon when she went ice fishing (she put it back again though) and spent a day in the Reykjavik women's ice hockey team, just before their trip to the World Championships in New Zealand.

After all that activity, what we both fancied was a slap up meal, and Zoe invited the girls from the team to join us for a traditional Icelandic feast.
Unfortunately, as I think you can tell from my expression, the main course of rotten shark meat with side orders of pickled rams' testicles and boiled sheep heads wasn't to everyone's liking, though, not for the first time, we tried to put a brave face on it and wash down the grisly grub with lots of water!

For my solo trip to Cambodia, I faced another unusual feast – apparently deep-fried spiders are a great delicacy here. There certainly seemed to be a plentiful supply of them. They tasted a bit like crispy bacon, though I couldn't quite bring myself to eat the main body of the spider.

Cambodia is a magical country, still recovering from the terrible years when it was ruled by a ruthless dictator called Pol Pot. Together with my 15-year-old guide (who tells tourists he's called James Bond!), I was lucky enough to take a trip into the jungle on an elephant's back.

Blue Peter

Our destination – the remains of some of Cambodia's many ancient and fabulous temples.

I was amazed at the sight of this enormous tree whose roots were wrapped around part of the structure – it looked like a set from a science fiction movie.

Whenever I've been on a Blue Peter filming trip, I can't wait to see the results and, once I was away from the dense greenery and out on the water on another fishing trip, I had time to reflect on how lucky I am to be able to see the world and share it with you.

Win a Day with Blue Peter

Yes, you really can win a trip to London to visit the Blue Peter studio. It's a prize money can't buy.

The lucky winner from our Book 34 competition was 11-year-old Heena Muhammed from Preston. Here she is sitting on the Blue Peter sofa with the presenters. She also tried her hand at operating one of our studio cameras and sat in the gallery with the director. She said it was the trip of a lifetime.

Would you like a chance to meet the presenters, pat the pets and visit the Blue Peter garden? If the answer is yes, then this is the competition for you.

This photograph was taken on Gethin's first appearance in the studio. Gethin is Batman the Caped Crusader but which super heroes are Konnie, Matt, Liz and Zoe dressed up as? If you can name them all, send your answer together with your name, age, address and telephone number to:

Blue Peter Day Out
BBC Television Centre
London W12 7RJ

The winner will be invited to spend the day with us and we'll provide the transport costs for a friend and family too (a maximum of four people). Photographs will be taken of the day and could feature in next year's annual.

Competition entries must be received by 28th February 2006. The winner will be notified by post no later than 30th April 2006 and the visit date will then be agreed.

RULES

1 Entrants must be under 16.

2 One winner will be chosen at random from the correct entries and will be notified by post.

3 The judges' decision will be final and no correspondence can be entered into.

4 Employees (and their relatives) of Pedigree and the BBC are not eligible to enter.

5 The compeititon is open to residents of the UK, Ireland and the Channel Islands.

6 The publishers reserve the right to vary the prize, subject to availability.

Blue Peter

Matt Baker

I've had a bit of a musical Blue Peter year, all things considered. There was my big challenge to write a Christmas song and, while I was making that, I got to interview one of the living legends of music, Madonna. We chatted about everything from wrestling (I'd just got back from my Sporting USA trip) to shoes, and she seemed delighted with her Blue Peter badge.

Back in the studio, I paid tribute to another music legend, Cole Porter, who wrote countless classic tunes. My dancing partner was Anna Kumble from Xchange.

Liz joined me for my second number – Porter's famous "Who Wants to be a Millionaire?" – which gave ITV the title for their hit quiz show.

As well as making music, I got to dance to it too – and on the day of our Alpine special, I actually had to show our guests Barney and Lizo from CBBC how to do the traditional lederhosen dancing I'd learnt in Austria. For the live show we were surrounded by experts who had flown in just for the show but we didn't let this put us off. We just slapped away for all we were worth. Only on Blue Peter!

Christmas Fairies

All you need to make a Christmas tree topper like this festive fairy is:

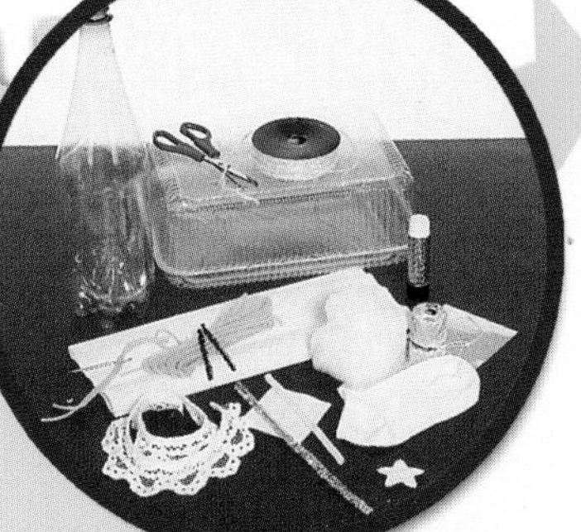

- A plastic bottle
- An old sock
- Cotton Wool or toy stuffing
- Needle and thread
- String
- Crepe paper
- Pipe cleaners
- Clear plastic container
- Wool
- Silver card
- Lace or fluffy trim

1. Cut the bottom off a tall drinks bottle. This will become the body.

2. Cut off the toe end from a sock and stuff with a little cotton wool to form the head.

3. Push the neck into the top of the bottle with the long end of string hanging down inside. Secure the string with some sticky tape on the inside of the bottle.

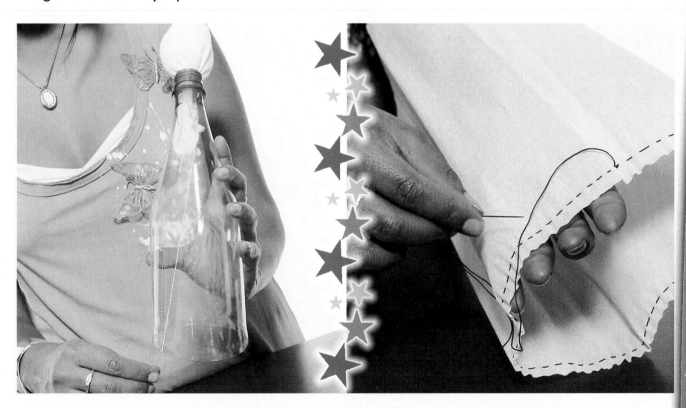

4. Cut a rectangle of crepe paper the height of your bottle and 45cm wide. Glue the 2 shorter edges together to from a tube and use a needle and thread to sew around one end. Pull the thread to gather the crepe paper dress. Place it over the bottle body, tightening the thread around the neck. Put a few stitches through the neck to keep the dress firmly in place.

5. The arms are also made from crepe paper. Cut two pieces 4 x 14cm. Cut two lengths of pipe cleaner 12cm long and cut two hand shapes from felt or from the leftover sock. Glue the hand to one end of the sleeve and lay the pipe cleaner on top. Spread glue along one side of the sleeve and wrap it around the arm. Glue the top of the sleeve to the top of the fairy's dress. Make a second arm and glue it opposite the first arm.

6. The hair is wool cut into 22cm lengths. Use a darning needle to thread two lenghts at a time through the head from one side to the other. You will probably need around 20 lengths. Wind a short length of pipe cleaner around the hair to form pigtails.

7. The wings are created by cutting a butterfly shape from a clear plastic container (ours held doughnuts). Spread glue around the edges of the wing shape and decorate with glitter. Allow the glitter to dry before bending the wings so that thay will stick out away from the fairy's body. Wrap a length of pipe cleaner around the centre of the wings and use it to attach them to the neck.

8. Make a crown from some silver card and glue in place.

9. Draw a face with markers or if you prefer, use stickers. Add lace or fluffy trim around the hem of the dress and a little around the neck.

10. A pipe cleaner with a tiny star glued to one end makes a wand. Glue it to the hand and she'll be ready to put on top of the Christmas tree.

Your fairy doesn't have to go on top of a tree – she'll look great on a bookshelf or mantelpiece.

HIGHLAND fling

If you go on holiday somewhere you really like, you might decide to make a return visit. But I shouldn't think there are many families who have been going on holiday to the same place for over 150 years! That's exactly what the Royal Family have done almost every year since 1852. Their destination is this fairytale castle – Balmoral in Scotland.

It was our Queen's great-great-grandmother, Queen Victoria and her husband Prince Albert who made Balmoral a royal holiday home. They loved the fresh air and wild countryside here, and Prince Albert pored over the plans for the castle and took a great interest in every detail of the new building.

Queen Victoria spent many happy hours sketching her favourite views. She wrote: "We have been so especially happy here. I seldom walk less than four hours a day and, when I come in, I feel as if I want to go out again…!"

Here the Royal Family could relax and forget the demands of their formal life in London – which is exactly why Balmoral is still popular with the Royal Family today.

In the ballroom, I was fascinated by this luxurious cot – made for one of Victoria's children. My baby Dexter would never experience anything quite so grand!

When Prince Albert died, aged only 42, Victoria was heartbroken. The grief remained with her for the rest of her long life – and Balmoral became a place to escape. She built impressive monuments to her dead husband. This one shows him wearing the kilt that he helped to make fashionable.

After my visit, I wasn't surprised that the Royal Family – the most talked about, photographed and filmed family in the world – still enjoy their annual break there. As Queen Victoria herself said: "Every year I seem to become fonder of this dear place. All seemed to breathe freedom and peace and to make one forget the world and its sad turmoil…."

Just nine miles away from Balmoral is the pretty town of Braemar. It is home to the world's most famous Highland Games, which is a bit like a giant sports day of traditional Scottish contests and events. Queen Victoria often visited Braemar, and since her death it's become a royal tradition for the reigning King or Queen to attend the games too. This year we were there as well, not as tourists but to take part.

Matt had a go at throwing the stone. It was a lot heavier than it looked so he didn't throw it very far!

Throwing the hammer is a skilled business too. You swing it around your head and project it as far as possible. Like Matt and the stone, Simon's best effort fell far short of the experts.

Next, both boys tried tossing the caber. These beauties weigh a staggering 60 kilos – the same weight as Matt – and you're supposed to toss it at least five metres away from you. They struggled just to lift the thing!

Sadly, as I was pregnant, I couldn't try any of the games. But I did enjoy the sights and sounds of all the Highland music, dancing and processions which carried on throughout the day. And of course I shouted myself hoarse cheering the boys on in the tug of war.

We had an exhausting – but brilliant – day, and we could see exactly why a trip to the Braemar Games is still a highlight of the Queen's holiday.

4000 AND

14th March 2005 – the day we celebrated 4000 episodes of Blue Peter – was always going to be a special one. Or was it? We'd noticed that, although the programme has been running since October 1958, we didn't have an accurate record of exactly how many episodes there have been.

Lucy Morris, who helps to run our Film Team, volunteered for the marathon task of painstakingly going through every one so we'd know exactly where we were. A few weeks later, she'd calculated that in fact we were about 80 episodes out – and that our 4000th edition was just a few weeks away.

On the day itself, we decided to start the show by arriving in style in a gigantic oversized shopping trolley!

COUNTING

Then we met our very special guest, Hollywood actor, Star Wars star, and lifelong Blue Peter fan, Ewan McGregor. Ewan told us he'd won a badge as a child for sending in his own bird cake recipe.

He was thrilled when we awarded him with a gold badge for his charitable work. After the show, he proudly wore his badge to the premiere of his new film!

He wasn't the only one getting his gold badge that day. Liz nipped out of the studio to meet England football hero, David Beckham and award him one too, for all his achievements in the game. Like Ewan, David grew up watching Blue Peter and says he was inspired to start football training after seeing an item on the programme.

As if all that wasn't enough, we welcomed the cast of smash hit musical, Mary Poppins, who wowed us with a performance of Supercallifragilisticexpialidocious.

It really was a great day – and all thanks to a lot of adding up!

Zöe

Zoe Salmon

When I look back at everything that's happened to me over the last few months, I can hardly believe it. My journey to join Blue Peter started when I spotted an advert in my local paper, the Belfast Telegraph. It said: "Can you act, sing and dance? Are you good at sport? Are you brave, intelligent, witty and hardworking? Could you cope with the pressure of TV? Could you interview anybody? Above all, can you be yourself?"

I made a tape and sent it in. A few days later, the phone rang – it was Blue Peter inviting me to London for an interview. It was the beginning of a gruelling audition process which took weeks and ended with me undergoing the famous trampoline test in the Blue Peter studio. The idea is that when you're bouncing up and down on a trampoline, a bit of the real you is bound to come out!

I was incredibly nervous but just tried to do my very best. At long last, I was invited to meet Blue Peter's Editor, who greeted me with champagne. I'd got the job!

People keep asking me if it has turned out like I expected but, as I didn't know what to expect, I can't answer that! Every day has brought something different – from paddling through the freezing cold water of a wild water race to having my precious hair turned into a hat for a special fashion show. The toughest challenge so far has been the day I spent as a student teacher – my class were great, though it was hard keeping control. But, as I said on my first show, there's nothing I'm not prepared to try while I'm on Blue Peter.

Bean on Blue Peter...

We've had quite a few celebrity guests on the programme over the last year but, without doubt, one of the most memorable was Mr Bean. None of us is quite sure who thought it would be a good idea to let him have a go on a camera right at the start of the live show, but at least the terrible, shaky, out of focus shots he offered gave us an idea of the mayhem in store!

Once we'd dragged him away from the camera, he managed to completely upstage our yoga item, insisting it would be a good idea for his teddy to take part too.

Liz wasn't at all sure what to make of Mr Bean's attempts to hold a conversation with the yet to be born Dexter.

Matt tried to explain that Blue Peter badges have to be earned – which obviously got Mr Bean thinking.

He begged Simon to be allowed to help in that day's cook – cheesy bread and butter pudding.

But Simon soon regretted allowing Mr Bean into the kitchen. He all but ruined a delicious recipe!

At the end of the programme, Liz decided it was time to award a badge – but not to Mr Bean. She pinned it on his long-suffering teddy instead!

PS. If you turn over, Gethin will show you how to make this mouth-watering teatime treat – with no interruptions!

Cheesy Bread & Butter Pudding

To make this quick, easy and tasty meal gather together the following ingredients:

- 6 Slices of white bread (stale bread works really well)
- 20g Butter
- Marmite
- 100g Grated Cheddar cheese
- 3 eggs
- 250ml Semi-skimmed milk
- Freshly ground pepper

You will need a medium sized ovenproof dish.

1. Butter the bread and then spread on a little Marmite. Cut the slices of bread into four.

2. Lightly beat the eggs and add the milk.

3. Whisk the mixture and season with some freshly ground black pepper.

4. Dip each piece of bread into the egg mixture and cover the base of the ovenproof dish. Sprinkle this layer with some of the grated cheese and follow with another layer of bread and more cheese until both are used up.

5. Pour any remaining egg mixture over the top.

6. Put in an oven pre-heated to gas mark 4 or 180C and let it bake for 30 minutes until the cheesy bread and butter pudding has turned golden on top.

Serve with cherry tomatoes or baked beans. People who say they hate Marmite could be converted after a mouthful of this savoury dish!

A Taste Of India

Our summer expedition to India was our most ambitious trip in years. We spent four weeks exploring the second most populated country in the world – with over one billion people – about seventeen times the population of the UK. To film all the reports, we had to cover enormous distances, so it really was a trip of 'planes, trains and automobiles – with the occasional camel thrown in too!

This is us next to the world-famous Taj Mahal – or Crown Palace – in Agra. It took 22 years to build – all in honour of the memory of Mumtaz Mahal, beloved wife of one of the Mogul emperors who ruled India 400 years ago. Legend has it that after the skilled craftsmen had completed the building, their hands were cut off so they would never be able to copy it. But despite that gruesome thought, to this day this fabulous, magical building remains a haunting monument to eternal love.

Eighty per cent of people in India follow the Hindu religion and I was fascinated to discover that to them the cow is a sacred animal – meaning the cows are kings of the road and everyone else has to dodge around them.

In the Corbett National Park, at the foothills of the Himalayas, we were lucky enough to get close to these wonderful elephants. They are really awe-inspiring beasts, weighing up to four tonnes. There are 625 wild elephants here which the park rangers have to guard carefully against poachers who try to slaughter the elephants for their tusks.

Although India competes in all the major international sports, traditional games are still very popular. I had a go at mallakhamb, a kind of Indian gymnastics. 'Malla' means 'man of strength' and 'khamb' means pole – and you can see why it got its name!

Kabaddi is a team sport. Over 4000 years old, it combines elements of wrestling and rugby in a game which is a bit like tag. It's great fun to play, even on a boiling hot day when you're four months pregnant!

The people of Rajasthan are known for their love of jewellery and bright colours. In Jaipur we had a go at cutting gemstones and block-printing saris, and ended the day modelling the finished look ourselves. We thought we looked all set to star in our own Bollywood spectacular!

In the capital city, New Delhi, the streets are over-run with literally thousands of Rhesus monkeys. Originally, the monkeys lived in the countryside, but they soon realised it was easier to find food in the big city. Unfortunately they can carry disease and be dangerous - and I joined Goli who, guided by his owner, helps to scare the monkeys away. Better than poisoning them, but a bit like painting the Forth Bridge - it's a job that never ends!

There are loads of links between Britain and India. When I was granted an audience with the Maharaja of Jodphur, one of India's ancient royal families, I discovered he had gone to school in England. Meanwhile, Simon explored the magnificent Mehrangarh Fort which dominates Jodphur and which was built to protect the wealth of the Maharajas.

The river Ganges is a vital lifeline for the people of Varanassi and many of them think of it as sacred.

Our journey into the Thar desert took the incredible heat we'd been experiencing to new extremes. We went as far as we could by road before switching over to a camel train. The camels were nice and steady, but they had appalling breath! We were spending a couple of days in the desert with Kaluna and his nomadic family. Before we could settle down to camp overnight, Simon had to help with a very important job – clearing the area of snakes. He'd been keen to have a go at this – funnily enough, no-one stood in his way!

We'd need a whole book to tell the full story of our expedition to India, but we hope we've given you some flavour of our journey to this colourful and unforgettable country.

INDIA

Photographic Memories

If you've got favourite happy snaps and holiday souvenirs that you'd like to keep safe, these photo frames are just the thing. You can show off your picture, and small keepsakes can be safely stored at the back.

Cut out 2 rectangles of card from an empty cereal packet. You can make the frame any size you want so long as it is bigger than your photo. Mark another rectangle in the middle of one of the pieces of card – it should be a little smaller than the photo you want to display. Cut out this smaller rectangle.

If you want to decorate your frame with a beach scene, cut a piece of pale blue paper large enough to cover the top third of the front of the frame and glue in place. Wrap the edges neatly around the back and secure. Tear off a piece of darker blue paper and glue it on with the straight edge meeting the skyline.

Follow this with other shades of blue and wavy strips of white paper to look like the sea and surf. Glue the strips in place and keep wrapping them around the frame until it is covered.
Extra decorations are up to you. Tear clouds and seagulls from white paper or a sand dune from a scrap of sandpaper. Tiny shells glued on will really bring the scene to life.

Cover the back of the second rectangle of card in plain paper – this will become the back of the frame. Before joining the front and back of the frame, create enough space to slip photos in and out of the top by cutting 3 strips of card. Glue them onto the bottom and both sides of the back of the frame. Now glue the front and back of the frame together.

Find a small box to keep your other holiday snaps and souvenirs in. Cover it in paper to match the frame. Glue it onto the back of the frame so that it will act as a stand as well as a handy container.

Slip your photo in and put the frame in pride of place!

And pop your keepsakes safely in the back!

Zoe's First Day

5th January 2005 is a day I'll remember for the rest of my life. I'd been introduced to viewers on the Christmas programme, but this was my first regular live show.

0900
I arrived at the BBC Television Centre studios in West London. There are 10 studios here, all of different sizes. Today Blue Peter was using the biggest - Studio One!

0905
Collecting my dressing room key from Stage Door, as Television Centre's reception is called. Just time to dump my bag as I was due in the dub.

Blue Peter

0945 Script in hand, Blue Peter Editor Richard Marson took me over to the studio for the start of camera rehearsals...

1000 Carmella Milne, the Floor Manager, is in charge of the studio floor – so she's very important. Here she is just about to cue me to start speaking.

0915 Dubbing Theatre Y. This is where we add the voice-overs to all of our Blue Peter films. Each line is carefully timed to fit the pictures – but it needs to sound natural too.

1010 The view you don't normally get to see – Blue Peter usually has four cameras, each taking different shots of the action.

1030 Simon and I were running through the recipe we were doing that afternoon – a special New Year cake – and, as I love cooking, I really enjoyed myself!

GRAMS - FREE VERSION

Monday Team

I joined Konnie, Simon and Matt in the canteen and they did their best to laugh me out of my nerves!

1300

1230

The studio broke for lunch and I had a moment to go through what we'd been rehearsing and gather my thoughts.

Year with some happy news

me appeal. Have made it

All - S nami (inc ideas for raising money

T: Coming Up This M

The A to e - os and as ers

1400

Badge Hit (Konnie)

Z - 12th night facts an

1130

Clos

Slowly but surely, we 'blocked' or rehearsed through every part of the programme.

LEONIE POCOCK (with Mabel & Lucy)
MARINA CRAGG (with Smudge)
(see page iv for visitors)

Blue Peter

58

1530

During run through Richard, our Editor, sits in a special booth with the Producers, watching everything we do and making notes of any cuts or changes he thinks are needed.

1515

We need to be fully made up for run through – or dress rehearsal – the only time the whole programme is rehearsed in order.

Time to check what I was planning to wear on the show with Costume Designer, Debbie Roberts.

GRAMS - FREE VERSION

1600

The show was a bit too long and needed cutting. Richard passed on his changes to the Director and her team.

1620

Down in make-up, it was our turn for notes. Richard told me not to frown so much – "You're telling us good news, so give us a smile!"

I passed on Richard's word changes to Helen, who operates the prompting system on our cameras. Sometimes we have to remember the whole script but, as this was my first proper show, I was glad Helen would be there making sure the words we had to speak could be seen under each camera.

1635

Monkey Team

/Dir: Bridget

Brendan

4.   All - Back

5   All - **SOS**
     ideas

6   **VT**   oney

7   All -   of Zoe - inc
     phot   k viewers ques

8   **VT**   Hit (Konnie)

...EONIE POCOCK (with Mabel & Lucy)
...ARINA CRAGG (with Smudge)
ee page iv for visitors)

0845 ROS / 0930 DUB/
1115 STUD

We were on the air – live! No going back –
but I loved every minute of it, even when
the team showed some embarrassing
photos of me growing up. Thanks Mum!

1700

Off air! It went really well. Now I was offficially part of the team –
and my Blue Peter career had begun!

1725

Blue Peter

Liz Barker

When I found out I was expecting a baby, the last thing I wanted to do was leave Blue Peter. Luckily, they didn't want me to, so I got ready for the challenge of being the first person to present the show while looking after a little baby.

Like many other mothers, I worked right up until the last minute – or so I thought! Baby Dexter had other ideas. The waiting nearly drove me bonkers, but when he finally arrived at 10.30pm on 4th December 2004, it was all worth it – he was perfect in every way. Blue Peter viewers sent Dex and me loads of cards and presents, which made me and my husband very happy.

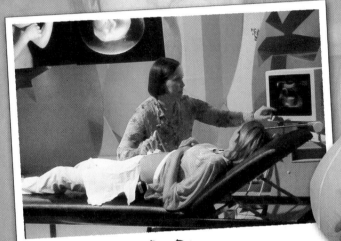

Having my scan live on Blue Peter...

Dexter has enjoyed all his trips to the Blue Peter studio. We've made a few film reports about his daily life too – and he takes it all in his stride. Perhaps all those months when I presented the show during my pregnancy were good training! I just think I'm lucky to have a job I love – and a wonderful little boy too.

My last show before Dex's birth

First trip to the studio

Dex at our Christmas show

Oh My Days!

I've always said that presenting Blue Peter was my dream job, so deciding to leave it was very difficult. I just felt that after six and a half very happy years, it was time to move on to new challenges and let someone else have a go at the best job in tv. I've visited 25 countries and appeared in an amazing 559 programmes. Here are a few shots from my Blue Peter photo album...

↗

This is me getting kitted up to try kite surfing on the Moroccan coast. I look the part - but I only got the kite up a few times!

↙

Learning to climb before my ascent on Mont Blanc was great fun - but it was a real test of my upper body strength.

I've been lucky enough to meet many of my sporting heroes like Olympic hero Amir Khan.

That's me under a thick layer of Dead Sea mud. Israel was a special trip for me because, as a Christian, it was a real thrill to report from the very place in which it's said that the baby Jesus was born.

In San Francisco, I climbed right to the top of the famous Golden Gate bridge. It's lucky I have a good head for heights!

I reported from Italy a few times. The Coliseum in Rome was the home of the bloody gladiator contests.

In Assisi in Italy, I spent two days dressed as St Francis, friend to the birds and the man behind the first Christmas crib.

Here I am as John Harrison, the genius who invented clocks that helped map the world. It was very windy when we filmed this and the hat kept flying off! ↘

↑ Dressing up and playing parts is all part of the job. This is me about to do battle as Oliver Cromwell.

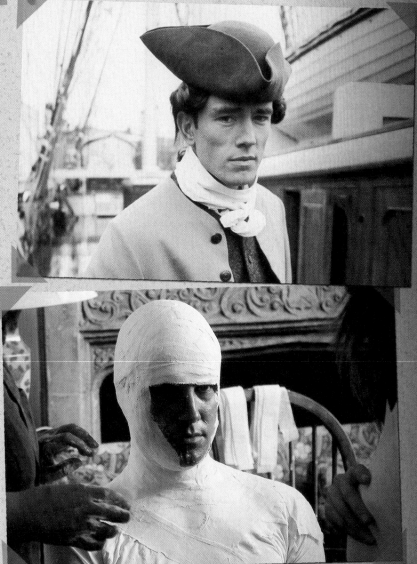

I've worn the kilt many times on Blue Peter and I really like it. In case you're wondering, I wore my footie shorts underneath it!

One of my most bizarre moments was being turned into a living statue during our adventure serial The Quest. I enjoyed filming these adventures - but not when they clashed with the football!

Congratulations if you recognise me as veteran crooner Cliff Richard. Ask your Mums!

I think what I'll miss most about Blue Peter is the sheer variety. One day, you might be in line being inspected as part of an elite army regiment…

← … the next you're baring your chest, singing and dancing in one of our special Christmas shows…

… or presenting Her Majesty the Queen with a gold badge!

Not quite an Oscar - but one of the many souvenirs I'll take and treasure as I look back over six of the best years of my life.

SPORTING USA

This is me getting ready to grapple with wrestling, one of the fast-paced sports I'd been sent to try out for a series of special Blue Peter reports. My destination was America, where colleges and high schools devote much time, training and huge amounts of hard cash to the big ones – baseball, basketball and American football. As you can see, I got kitted up and tried them all, but I think the one that sticks in my mind most of all was wrestling.

Wrestling is one of the world's oldest sports. The folk style or collegiate wrestling which is popular in the States is nothing like the WWE wrestling you may have seen on tv. Most of that is staged, but this is the real deal. I guess it's the fact that it's so simple that makes it so exciting – standing face to face with your opponent with only your bare hands to fight them with gives you a huge adrenalin rush. But the outfit didn't help – it's designed so your opponent has as little to grab hold of as possible.

I was told that my gymnastic background would be useful because balance, strength and flexibility are all really important, but that I would need to be really aggressive to stand a chance of winning. Not surprising when you consider that my opponent was Scott Moore. That season, Scott was ranked the number one wrestler in the USA for his weight category – winning a staggering 54 of his 63 bouts. I was right to be nervous!

The ear protectors were a comfort but, as I squared up to Scott, I had a feeling that my best efforts wouldn't be enough to pin him down.

Scott was giving nothing away. He knew that I was a beginner, so he played with me a bit and let me try a few moves before he started to show me just why he's a champion. In seconds, I was pressed on to the mat, completely unable to move.

Then he began to play with me like a cat with a mouse. The holds he used were agony – and I really hurt my shoulder. Sweating, aching, limbs like jelly – it was all over in a few minutes.

And then Scott turned into a really nice guy, generously telling me that I hadn't done too badly after all. I smiled weakly and hobbled off to get changed, wondering if I ought to see a physio about my aching shoulder.

Gethin Jones

April 26th 2005 – a day I'll never forget. My nail-biting first appearance as presenter number 31 and the end of a very long journey indeed!

I used to watch Blue Peter round at my Auntie Jean's house, eating bananas and custard – but I thought that presenting it could only ever be a dream. When I grew up, I went to University in Manchester and then started working on tv in Wales. I ended up on a show called Uned 5, very like a Welsh language Blue Peter – and after two years on that, I decided the time was right to try my luck in London. I sent a tape to CBBC and that got me a chance to visit Blue Peter's Editor for a chat and a look round the studio.

A few months later, I got the call to audition. I thought the audition went okay, but I knew there would be a wait. I was right – it was three months before I finally discovered I'd got the job. In fact, by the time I arrived on screen, a year had passed since that first visit to the studio. Was it worth the wait? You bet!

I can't believe how much I've crammed in already. I've got my pilot's licence, and so the chance to fly in a helicopter over Niagara Falls in America was just one of my early memorable moments.

Perhaps it was my love of flying that gave somebody the idea to dress me up as Batman on my first show. The costume was made of rubber and apart from being boiling hot, it smelt like a pair of old wellies!

Right at the end of my first show, the team reunited me with my faithful toy horse, Neddy. I'm a bit too big for him these days, but I had a ride for old times' sake. Embarrassing school photos, smelly costumes and toy horses – what a way to begin…

I didn't mind of course – I was just so happy to be here.

SUPER SMUDGE

On September 14th 2004 an inquisitive bundle of ginger and white fur padded into the Blue Peter studio and faced a posse of press photographers jostling to get a picture of the latest member of the team. Our new kitten had arrived and it was love at first sight. But he needed a name and more than 15,000 viewers sent in their ideas. Smudge was very popular because of the little patch of ginger fur beside his pink nose – and that's the name we gave him.

It was a tall order to replace Kari and Oke who had been the feline rulers of the studio for 13 years but Smudge took it all in his stride. Many kittens had been seen but Blue Peter wanted a very special one. Apart from being good looking, intelligent and sweet natured, it would have to like being handled. When we heard about a cat and her litter of five kittens that were all needing homes we went to investigate. They were all adorable but the ginger and white one had stardom written all over him.

Blue Peter

Just like any responsible pet owner, we arranged for Smudge to have all his innoculations. He had his booster jab and was microchipped in the studio in front of millions of viewers. He gave a little whimper and soon forgot all about needles as he tried the weighing scales for size.

In December, Smudge was one of the star attractions at the National Cat Club Show. He was lucky enough to sample some of the cat toys that were on sale there. Smudge soon made himself at home in a cosy cheese-shaped bed which we wrapped and kept until Christmas. He still loves snuggling up inside it and another of his passions is water, he likes nothing better than playing with a dripping tap. Another of his hobbies is watching TV – especially Blue Peter.

Just like any young cat Smudge is full of fun and mischief. Now he has even more Blue Peter friends and has taken a particular shine to Gethin who thinks Smudge is "a real cool cat"!

If you'd like to make your own mini Smudge, turn the page and follow the instructions...

Blue Peter

75

Mini SMUDGE

If you'd like to make a Mini Smudge, it's not easy but the end result is well worth the effort! His coat is soft white fleece but you could use towelling, and his body is filled with split peas.

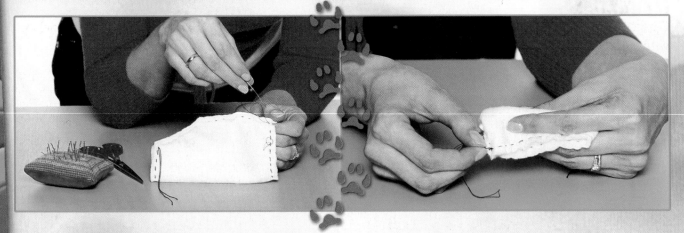

Start by making a pattern for the body. Use a piece of paper 20 x 15 cm and fold it in half widthways. Cut off the top corners from the unfolded side and this will make the shape of the body as it narrows towards the neck.

Pin the paper pattern on to white material and cut out this shape.

Fold the material in half (wrong side out) and sew the shaped side together using fairly small stitches. You will end up with a tube.

Do not sew across the top or the bottom of the tube but sew all the way around using straight stitches and leave the thread loose.

Pull the thread on the wider end of the body shape first and when the material has gathered tightly, oversew or tie the thread ends into a knot.

Blue Peter

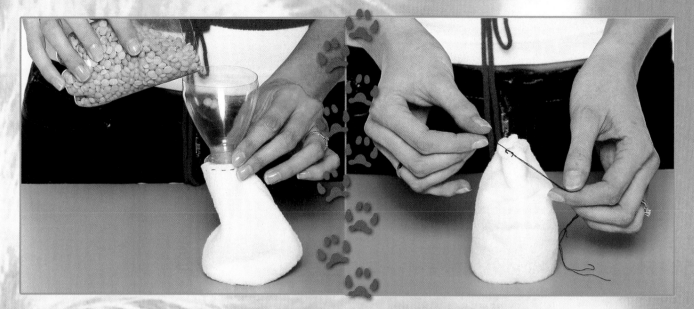

Turn the material right side out and you'll be ready to fill the body with split peas. To make the job easier, cut off the top section of a plastic bottle to make a funnel. Push the bottle neck into the open section of the body and pour in the peas. Fill the body nearly to the top and then pull up the loose thread and knot or oversew to keep the peas securely inside.

Again make a paper pattern for the head. Cut out a circle of paper measuring 11.5 cm across. Fold the paper in half and then cut off about a third.

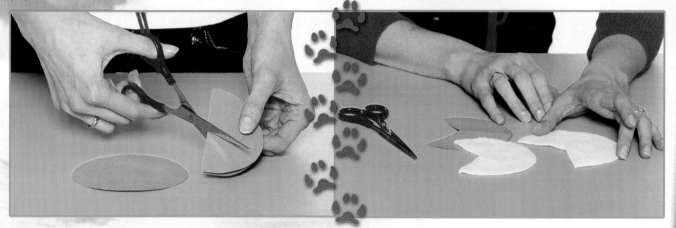

Open out this paper pattern and pin it on a double thickness of white material and cut out. You'll end up with two shapes.

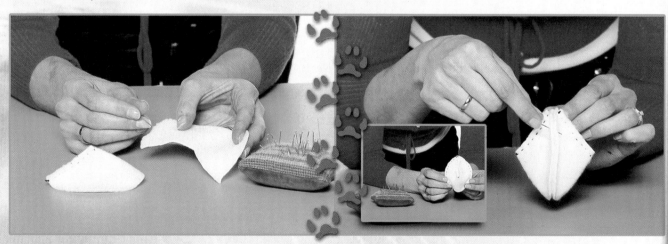

Stitch the straight edges together on the first head section and repeat on the other.

Joining the two pieces is tricky so take your time. Match up the joins and pin. Carefully stitch the two pieces together leaving a gap at the bottom to put the peas in.

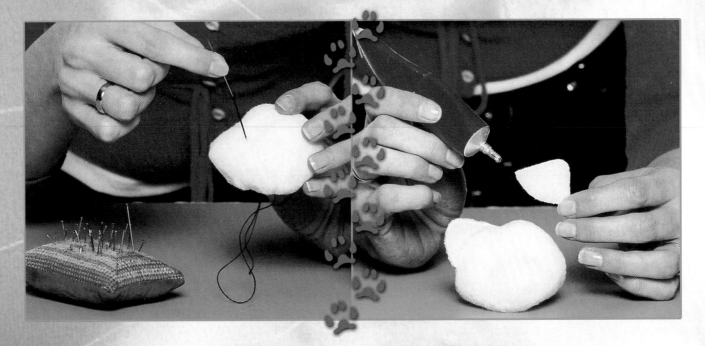

Turn the head right side out and fill with peas. Gather and sew up the opening in the same way as for the body. To give Mini Smudge's face a shape sew through from the gathered end to where an eye would be and then push the needle back again to the gathering. Pull the thread tightly and oversew. Repeat for the second eye.

Ears are fan shaped pieces of material with the bottoms rounded off. Cut out a pair and attach to the head with glue or tiny stitches. Next, glue or sew the head on the body stitches with the seam at the back.

Front legs are 2 oblongs of material 7 x 10 cm long. Fold the long sides to the middle then sew or glue the folded edges together to make long, tube shapes. Tuck in the edge at one end and then gather up with a few stitches to make paw shapes. Put some split peas or toy stuffing into the front legs for shape then sew up the ends. Fix the tops of the legs to the front of the body with a little gap between them. The back legs are made in the same way from 2 oblongs of material 7cm x 5 cm but they do not need stuffing. Fix under the body so that the paws show either side of the front legs.

The tail is another oblong of material about 7cm x 11 cm tapering off at one end. Make in the same way as the legs but make the tip as small as possible. Fix the straight end of the tail at the back of the body.

Use a marker pen to lightly add Smudge's ginger markings. Work from the middle to the edges and add more colour if you need to. Don't forget the little smudge around his nose!

His nose is a tiny piece of pink material shaped like a quarter circle with the point cut off. Make whiskers from strands of sewing thread tied in the middle, then glue them on to the back of the nose and attach to the face with glue. Eyes are split peas painted black then glued onto tiny circles of green paper.

Make a collar from a length of ribbon. Smudge's name disc is a pink heart which is cut from pink card. Sew it onto the ribbon then wrap the collar around the neck and secure.

Mini Smudge looks just like the genuine article and he's right at home with the rest of Blue Peter's mini pets which we have made over the past few years. We hope you'll have as much fun making mini pets as we have.

GET SOME IN!

Sixty years ago, after the end of the Second World War, it was decided to introduce National Service. This meant that if you were aged 18 to 26, you had to 'get some in!' and spend two years in the Army, Navy or Air Force. To find out what it was like, we enlisted Privates Baker, Matthew and Jones, Gethin.

Like most young men of the time, they reported for their new life in civilian clothes.

But their 'civvies' didn't last long. Soon they were loaded up with all kinds of new kit. "If it fits, you must be deformed", they were told.

Long hard hours were spent on drill – learning to obey commands instantly and in time.

Blue Peter

Standards were high, as Private Jones found out when an Officer used a piece of paper to test how well Jones had shaved.

Inspections were frequent and there were all kinds of punishments or 'jankers' for failure.

These ranged from extra physical exercise...

... to peeling endless piles of potatoes...

... and even to cutting the grass with nail scissors. National Service was tough and you soon learnt to do as you were told.

Blue Peter

Physical fitness was important and you had to be really ill to get out of it – a cold was no excuse!

Boxing was very popular – even if you had to fight your mates, you went for it – or else!

These young men were being trained to kill and they had to show real aggression.

What little spare time they had was spent in the NAAFI – a canteen where they could enjoy a cup of tea, a smoke and a sing-song.

Young men from very different backgrounds often ended up lifelong friends.

After basic training, they could be posted all over the world. National Service was an experience they would all remember for the rest of their lives – a time when they grew up, became men and made unbreakable friendships in the service of their country.

THE (TEA) TIME LORD

From the 1960s to the 1980s, the science fiction adventure series, Doctor Who, was a Saturday teatime tradition, with generations of children hiding behind the sofa from the often terrifying monsters the Doctor battled. Then the Doctor, a Time Lord from the planet Gallifrey, vanished from our screens. Until now that is. The ninth and latest Doctor, played by Chris Eccleston, arrived in the Blue Peter studio in his trusty TARDIS – a space ship disguised as a 1960s police box.

POLICE PUBLIC CALL BOX

He didn't come alone either. There was the somewhat alarming Face of Boe, an alien head in a giant tank.

Chris let me try on the Doctor's leather jacket, which was pretty cool. I'd actually been lucky to film on the set of the new series too.

That's where I met
one of the Doctor's oldest
and deadliest enemies,
the Dalek!

Back in our studio, we showed Chris a
Dalek made by two Blue Peter viewers.
It's actually a giant compost bin so, instead
of exterminating the Earth, it helps
to regenerate it!

Chris also admired some
fantastic models sent in by
fans of the show.

Doctor Who's
return to BBC1
has been a big success
and, although Chris won't
be playing the Doctor in the
2006 series, we think it's brilliant
that the Doctor's incredible
adventures in time and space
have made Saturday night
television exciting
again!

Blue Peter

WELCOME HOME

We know how much Blue Peter viewers are capable of, but little did we realise when we launched our Welcome Home Appeal last November just how magnificently you'd respond. We were working with the Red Cross, who'd told us about the terrible situation in Angola in Africa, where a 29-year-old civil war has torn the country apart and split up thousands of families. Trying to trace your loved ones in a country almost without roads (and those that are left are laced with landmines) and with no modern communications is literally like trying to find a needle in a haystack. We asked you to imagine the agony of knowing your parents or children might be alive somewhere with no way of finding them.

We wanted to raise money to help fund the long, painstaking process of reuniting families. The money would pay for everything from tracing posts, where people can register to find loved ones, to starter kits for anyone returning to their family, to help with the expense.

We asked you to collect bags of used clothing, which the Red Cross would sort and sell in their shops right across the UK. We estimated that each bag might raise around £10 and we set our target at 25,000 bags. Could you do it?

Actionline: 0870 833 5000

Within two weeks of launching our appeal, you could and did. We raised the target to 50,000 bags – and by the first week in January, you'd smashed that too. In fact, as we went to press on this book, the number of bags you'd collected was a staggering 108,000.

We can never say enough thank yous, but we hope that seeing just some of the photos of the people you helped return to their families will be a reminder of how you have helped to bring happiness back into a lot of Angolan people's lives.

RHINOMANIA

THIS IS ME AT CHESTER ZOO WITH ONE OF THEIR SEVEN CRITICALLY ENDANGERED BLACK RHINOS. TODAY WE'RE LUCKY THAT IT'S EASY TO GET A GOOD CLOSE-UP LOOK AT RARE AND BEAUTIFUL ANIMALS LIKE THESE. BUT JUST IMAGINE THE SENSATION CAUSED WHEN PEOPLE IN EUROPE CAUGHT SIGHT OF A RHINOCEROS FOR THE VERY FIRST TIME. THIS IS THE STORY OF RHINOMANIA.

IT WAS 1741. A BABY RHINO WAS BORN IN ASSAM IN NORTH-EAST INDIA, BUT WHEN SHE WAS ONLY ONE MONTH OLD, HER MOTHER WAS KILLED BY HUNTERS AND SHE WAS ORPHANED.

SHE WAS RESCUED BY A MR SICHTERMAN, WHO LIVED NEARBY. HE CALLED THE LITTLE RHINO CLARA. TO IMPRESS HIS DINNER GUESTS, SICHTERMAN TRAINED CLARA TO SIT AT HIS DINNER TABLE, WHERE SHE AMAZED GUESTS BY EATING DAINTILY FROM A PLATE.

THEN A VISITING DUTCH SEA CAPTAIN CALLED VAN DER MEER OFFERED TO BUY CLARA AND TAKE HER WITH HIM TO EUROPE.

DURING THE LONG SEA VOYAGE, CLARA LIVED ON DECK IN A SPECIALLY BUILT CAGE COVERED WITH A CANVAS SUN SHADE. THE SAILORS GAVE HER BEER TO DRINK, WHICH SHE LOVED, ALTHOUGH IT DIDN'T ALWAYS AGREE WITH THEM!

VAN DER MEER HAD BIG PLANS FOR CLARA. HE DECIDED TO TAKE HER ON A 'GRAND TOUR' OF EUROPE AND SO HE HAD A SPECIAL TRAVELLING COACH BUILT CAPABLE OF CARRYING A THREE TONNE RHINOCEROS.

OVER THE YEARS THAT FOLLOWED, CLARA AND VAN DER MEER JOURNEYED TOGETHER ACROSS THOUSANDS OF MILES. NOBODY COULD SNEAK A FREE LOOK AT CLARA BECAUSE THE COACH ONLY HAD TINY WINDOWS!

Blue **Peter**

IN THOSE DAYS, MANY PEOPLE THOUGHT RHINOS WERE JUST A MYTH, SO WHEREVER SHE WENT, SHE CAUSED A SENSATION. EVERY DAY, CROWDS PAID FOR THEIR TURN TO WONDER AT THIS EXTRAORDINARY ANIMAL.

MEANWHILE VAN DER MEER DID A ROARING TRADE SELLING SOUVENIRS AND PICTURES OF CLARA SO THAT PEOPLE COULD REMEMBER THEIR CLOSE ENCOUNTER WITH RHINOMANIA.

THE CROWDS ESPECIALLY LOVED IT WHEN SHE DISPLAYED HER GENTLE NATURE BY LICKING VAN DER MEER'S FACE WITH HER LONG TONGUE.

HER APPEARANCE STARTED A CRAZE FOR ALL THINGS RHINOCEROS. FASHIONABLE LADIES EVEN TOOK TO WEARING THEIR HAIR 'A LA RHINOCEROS' - PILED UP WITH A FAKE HORN IN FRONT!

Blue Peter

CLARA ARRIVED IN VENICE ON A MASSIVE BARGE, CAUSING A FEVER OF EXCITEMENT. BY NOW, SHE HAD MADE VAN DER MEER A RICH MAN AND THEY TOURED EUROPE TOGETHER FOR 17 LONG YEARS.

IT WAS IN LONDON THAT CLARA DIED ON APRIL 14TH 1758, BUT HUNDREDS OF YEARS AFTER HER DEATH, CLARA'S STORY LIVES ON; A GENTLE AND MAGNIFICENT ANIMAL WHO BROUGHT EXCITEMENT, SENSATION - AND RHINOMANIA - TO EUROPE.

FROM MY OWN CLOSE ENCOUNTER WITH THE RHINOS OF CHESTER ZOO, I CAN QUITE SEE WHY CLARA MADE SUCH AN IMPACT. RHINOS TRULY ARE FABULOUS ANIMALS AND IF YOU EVER FANCY A GOOD CLOSE-UP LOOK YOURSELF, BLUE PETER BADGE WINNERS GET INTO CHESTER ZOO ABSOLUTELY FREE!

Blue Peter

Jones the Butler

If you're rich, royal, famous – or all three - having your own butler is a must. A butler is the central figure in all grand households. They are usually impressive and imposing men whose job is to make sure the lives of their masters run like clockwork and that their every need is seen to. A hundred years ago, every large household had a butler – nowadays they are much more unusual and their skills mean they are in great demand. Good butlers can work all over the world and they are very well rewarded for their special service.

I trained under Ashley Powell at the Ivor Spencer School for Butlers. First, Ashley taught me the vital importance of my appearance – nails short and clean, hair tidy (mine was too long, apparently) and uniform spotless with the tie perfectly knotted.

Then I tried some of a butler's many demanding duties – from ironing the newspaper so that the ink doesn't come off on your master's hands…

… to seeing to every detail of your master's home and belongings. As I discovered, there's no substitute for elbow grease and good old spit and polish.

After Ashley had shown me the correct way to lay out a table, I prepared for my big test – being butler to a VIP dinner.

The VIPs were both rather familiar – but I kept my mind on the job. A good butler tries to think about what the guests might want before they want it – whether it's more water or bread.

When I wasn't serving, I kept in the background. I had been taught that no butler joins in the conversation or speaks to the guests, unless he is spoken to first.

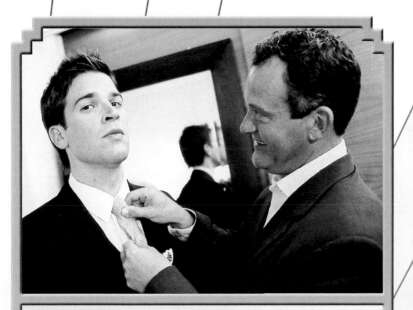

I thought I did quite well – but my challenge wasn't over yet. I was sent to meet Britain's most famous butler Paul Burrell, who worked for the royal family for 22 years and whom the late Princess Diana called her "rock". More recently, he starred in I'm a Celebrity, Get Me Out Of Here! The first thing Paul did was to check my tie!

Next he balanced a book on my head – could I walk tall without it falling off? It was tricky but it certainly helped me to hold myself well.

Finally Paul gave me a quiz – running through a fast-paced set of questions designed to test my knowledge of butlering to the limit.

"What side do you serve food on?" – (answer: the left),

"Would you normally have silver or china for lunch?" – (answer: china),

"Bottom button on your waistcoat done up or undone?" – (answer: undone)

I got them all right! Paul kindly said he was impressed. Although I was delighted, I remembered my training and didn't say a word – but inside, I reckoned that perhaps I had another career going if Blue Peter doesn't work out…!

Blooming Gorgeous!

Whatever you want to say – happy birthday, happy Easter or happy Mothers' Day – there's no better way than to say it with flowers! My idea for everlasting blooms in a pretty vase will save you pounds and is guaranteed to please.

All you need is:

- A small juice carton
- PVA Glue
- Paint
- Sawdust (available from pet shops)
- Thin wire
- Cereal packet
- Crepe paper
- Green card or paper
- Modelling clay
- Shredded tissue paper

Blue Peter

Cut the top off an empty juice carton. Rinse and dry the carton and cut away 3.5 cm from the sides.

Cut thin card from a cereal packet to cover the outside of the carton.

Draw and cut away curved shapes on both the front and the back of the carton.

To give the vase an unusual texture, mix together some paint, pva and a handful of sawdust. Make a fairly thick paste to cover all four sides of the carton. Allow 3 to 4 hours to dry. If you have any coloured jewels or beads these will look pretty glued on the top of the carton.

To make carnations, take a pack of folded crepe paper and make a cut through the whole thickness about 6cm wide.

Keep the strip of paper folded and carefully snip it into thin strips leaving about 1 cm uncut. Unravel and you will be left with a very long fringe. Cut this into roughly 20 cm lengths to make lots of flowers.

Take a length of thin wire about 20 cm long and cover with green crepe paper and glue the ends to make the stem.

Wind the crepe paper fringe around the top of the stem dabbing on a little glue as you go. Gently open out the petals and curve using the closed blades of scissors. Cover the base of the flower with a strip of pink or green paper. Cut leaves from green card, score down the centre and glue along the stem.

Make as many flowers as you like and push the stems into a lump of modelling clay before popping them into the decorated carton. Top up with shredded tissue paper and voilà – beautiful everlasting flowers! You can use the same idea to create different shaped vases and a whole host of multi-coloured flowers.

It's A Dog's Life!

Health clubs, gyms and spas for humans are nothing new – but what about one for pets? When we heard about the pet resort in Leeds, we decided to take our hard-working four-legged superstars – Mabel, Lucy and Meg – on a canine mini-break.

After we'd checked in, the first treat was an exercise class with Mary Ray, one of the UK's leading dog trainers. Mary put us all through a heel work to music class – a bit like aerobics for dogs. She suggested we choose a piece of music all the dogs were familiar with and Matt came up with Old Macdonald had a Farm.

It certainly did the trick for Meg, who soon got the idea and happily strutted her stuff...

But despite my best efforts to set a good example, Mabel, on the other hand, wasn't really into it at all.

Next it was time to pamper our pooches. First, a warm bath with shampoo followed by a blow dry from both sides.

Next, I'd booked Mabel in for a spot of hydrotherapy – basically swimming against an artificial current, which is supposed to help strengthen a dog's legs. Mabel is nearly 10 years old, and Linda from the resort told me that older dogs love this treatment and find it very relaxing. I certainly hoped so – she hadn't seemed all that impressed with the heel work, and this was her day out, after all.

When we'd helped her out of the pool, Mabel shook herself all over me – perhaps it was her revenge for getting her wet twice in one day? Oh well, she definitely seemed to have enjoyed herself!

Doga - or dog yoga – is the latest idea from (where else?) America – combining relaxation, stretching and breathing techniques to help your dog to chill out. It's also supposed to be a great way of bonding with your pet. After a few minutes, Mabel, Lucy and Meg certainly seemed to grow calmer and their breathing fell into the same rhythm as ours. I'd say this was the best part of the day for both dogs and humans.

Being a resort means that your dogs can stay here too – and we all got cosy in their personalised hotel room with its central heating, double glazing, toys and even a tv set. If we're honest, we're not sure that Mabel, Lucy and Meg are really that bothered about a life of luxury. Plenty of food, some good walks, and owners who love them to bits is what really counts, of course – but all the same, we'd enjoyed sharing our dogs' special day out.

Baker's Blueberry Muffins

To make foolproof muffins, gather together the following ingredients and you'll be all set to get baking!

- 60g Butter
- 115g Caster sugar
- 2 Medium eggs
- 250g Plain flour
- 2tsp Baking powder
- 125ml Milk
- 150g Blueberries
- Pinch of salt
- Muffin cases and tray

1. Cut the butter into small cubes. Put in a mixing bowl together with the caster sugar and use a wooden spoon to cream the two together.

2. Crack and add one egg, beating it into the mixture. When the egg has been absorbed, repeat the process with the second egg.

3. Put the flour, baking powder and a pinch of salt into another mixing bowl and gently sift together.

4. Then add small amounts of the dry flour mixture and the milk to the original mixture giving a good stir each time. Keep doing this until all the flour and milk has been used up and the muffin mixture is smooth.

5. Finally add the blueberries and stir well.

6. Line a tray with muffin cases and carefully spoon in the mixture. Only fill each case 3/4 full as the mixture will rise when cooked. There should be enough to make 10 muffins. If you have a smaller sized bun tray you'll make even more! Bake the muffins in an oven pre-heated to 180°c or gas mark 4 for roughly 25 minutes. Keep an eye on them and remove when they are golden brown. Leave the muffins to cool for around 20 minutes and then tuck in!

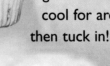

P.S. you can substitute cranberries, sultanas or chocolate chips for the blueberries if you prefer.

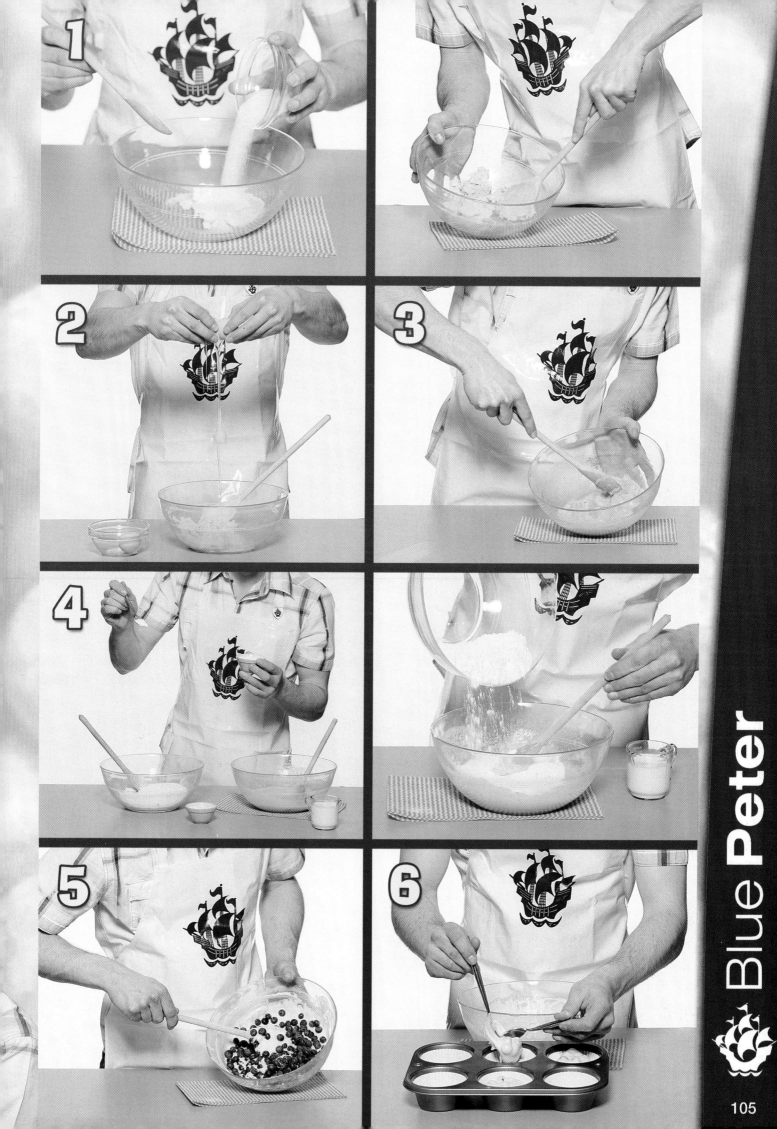

Dear Blue Peter...

Thousands of letters and emails pour into the Blue Peter office every week - it's great to see and hear what you've been up to. Keep writing to us as the chances are you'll earn yourself a badge. We also choose one star letter and photo to show at the end of Blue Peter and, if you're really lucky, **IT COULD BE YOU!**

My dad was cutting down some trees in our garden so me and my sister Sophie decided to make a shelter like you did. It took us ages and I don't think it will keep the rain out but we had fun building it! Thank you for the idea.
Love from
Abi & Sophie Abrahams
Ilminster, Somerset

...as seen on **TV!**

Here is a picture of me and the moneybox hedgehog I made. It is the most favourite thing I have ever made. Keep up the good work.
Love
Jessica Berry
Preston, Lancashire

Me and my brother have made a banana and walnut cake like you did on the show. It was delicious. Here is a photo of us and the finished cake. Yum, Yum!
From Rhiannon and Benjy Davies
Yeovil, Somerset

I really enjoy your show and specially like the animal bits. I also like making things and here is a photo of me and my brother with the Sewer for the Turtles as seen on Blue Peter.
From Elinor Webster
Cheshire

I enjoyed making Matt's Cock-a-Leekie pie so much that I am sending a photo of one I made earlier! Me and my family really, really enjoyed it and look forward to the next recipe.
From Blue Peter fan
Laura Hunt
Nottingham

I watch your show all the time and I never miss it. I used your advice for the Mother's Day flowers and took a picture of them. My mum loved them.
Blue Peter is the best.
From Aishah Khalid Saroya
London

...as seen on TV!

We really liked the plant pot make so we thought we would have a go at making them for presents. Here is a picture of the plant pots we made.
Laura and Polly Nicholson
Worthing, West Sussex

I have got a dog called Snip. He is a whippet. He is helping me to learn about taking care of our environment. Every week I collect his aluminium food tins and put them in the recycling box. When I take Snip for a walk, I look after the environment by cleaning up his dog mess. Not nice but very necessary!
Chris Carey
Hertfordshire

Now turn over to see how you can win a badge for yourself.

Have you got one?

Blue Peter badges were dreamt up way back in 1963 and over the years hundreds of thousands of children have won one of our coveted awards.

Today there are five Blue Peter badges and they are all special as they have to be won. Here's how you could do just that!

BLUE badges were the originals. The presenters wear them in the studio and when they are away filming. Send us an interesting letter, a good idea for the programme, a poem or a story and you could earn yourself a Blue badge.

SILVER is the badge you'll probably win after your Blue but you will have to do something different. For example, if you won your Blue for sending a programme idea, how about sending us a poem or a painting?

GREEN badges are awarded to viewers who tell us about environmental projects they are involved with or who write to us about any "green" subject.

COMPETITION badges are awarded to winners as well as runners up in Blue Peter competitions.

GOLD badges are our highest award. They are won for outstanding achievements like saving someone's life or extreme bravery. Some very famous people have also been presented with our highest award and recently these have included the brilliant author and illustrator Raymond Briggs, Olympic double gold medal winner Dame Kelly Holmes and England football captain, David Beckham.

If you can, send us a photograph with your letter as it may end up on the show or in next year's annual!

Blue Peter